AF322946

The
Christ Within
&
The Disciples of Christ

with the

Cosmic Christ Calendar

BOOKS BY JOHN-ROGER

Awakening Into Light
Baraka
Blessings of Light
The Consciousness of Soul
A Consciousness of Wealth
Dream Voyages
Drugs
Dynamics of the Lower Self
Forgiveness—Key to the Kingdom
God Is Your Partner
Inner Worlds of Meditation
The Journey of a Soul
Loving…Each Day
Manual on Using the Light
The Master Chohans of the Color Rays
Passage Into Spirit
The Path to Mastership
Possessions, Projections & Entities
The Power Within You
Q&A from the Heart
Relationships—The Art of Making Life Work
Sex, Spirit & You
The Signs of the Times
The Sound Current
The Spiritual Family
The Spiritual Promise
The Tao of Spirit
Walking with the Lord
The Way Out Book
Wealth & Higher Consciousness

CO-WRITTEN WITH PETER MCWILLIAMS
DO IT!
LIFE 101
You Can't Afford the Luxury of a Negative Thought
WEALTH 101
We Give to Love

FOR FURTHER INFORMATION, PLEASE CONTACT:
MSIA®
P.O. Box 3935, Los Angeles, CA 90051
(213) 737-4055

The
Christ Within
&
The Disciples of Christ

with the

Cosmic Christ
Calendar

JOHN-ROGER

Mandeville Press
Los Angeles, California

Published by Mandeville Press
P.O. Box 3935
Los Angeles, CA 90051

Printed in the United States of America

I.S.B.N. 0-914829-35-1

Contents

1

Jesus the Man, Jesus the Christ

ach year at Christmas time, much of humankind celebrates the birth of Jesus, who lived two thousand years ago and was brought forward and Christed in that dispensation. At this time of year, it is sometimes easier for us to tune in to the Christ within our own consciousnesses through remembering Jesus the Christ.

The Gospel of Luke beautifully tells the story of Jesus' birth:

> In those days a decree went out from Caesar Augustus that all the world should be enrolled.... And all went to be enrolled, each to his own city. And Joseph also went up from Galilee, from the city of Nazareth, to Judea, to the city of David, which is called Bethlehem, because he was of the house and lineage of David, to be enrolled with Mary, his betrothed, who was with child. And while they were there, the time came for her to be delivered. And she gave birth to her first-born son and wrapped him in swaddling cloths, and laid him in a manger, because there was no place for them in the inn.

And in that region there were shepherds out in the field, keeping watch over their flock by night. And an angel of the Lord appeared to them, and the glory of the Lord shone around them, and they were filled with fear. And the angel said to them, "Be not afraid; for behold, I bring you good news of a great joy which will come to all the people; for to you is born this day in the city of David a Savior, who is Christ the Lord. And this will be a sign for you: you will find a babe wrapped in swaddling cloths and lying in a manger." And suddenly there was with the angel a multitude of the heavenly host praising God and saying, "Glory to God in the highest, and on earth peace among men with whom he is pleased!"

When the angels went away from them into heaven, the shepherds said to one another, "Let us go over to Bethlehem and see this thing that has happened, which the Lord has made known to us." And they went with haste, and found Mary and Joseph, and the babe lying in a manger. And when they saw it they made known the saying which had been told them concerning this child; and all who heard it wondered at what the shepherds told them. But Mary kept all these things, pondering them in her heart. And the shepherds returned, glorifying and praising God for all they had heard and seen, as it had been told to them.[1]

Whether we read from the Revised Standard Version of the Bible, the classic King James Version, or the more modern

---

1. Luke 2:1-20 (Revised Standard Version)

Aquarian Gospel[2] it is always beautiful to read again the story of Jesus' birth into the physical world because it symbolizes for each of us the promise of our own divine heritage.

Many things have been said and written about this man, who was overshadowed by the Christ. Here was a man who had a perfect love relationship with the entire world, a perfect love. Can you imagine that perfect love with everything that existed? A story was told of Jesus walking down a road and coming upon the decaying carcass of a dog. It was the dog's teeth Jesus looked at, and he said, "Look how beautifully they shine." Others saw the decay and smelled the stench, but his perfect love saw only the perfect beauty. As we enter into our own Christ Consciousness within—and it is within each one of us—we are stirred into seeing this beauty as it is represented around us in this present time.

Here was a man who, in one moment, was so tender that the most beautiful music was coarse in comparison, yet who was also so rugged and stern that the mightiest oak tree was nothing compared to him. Can you imagine the dimension of someone who could come forward in one moment and cleanse a "marketplace" and, in the next moment, raise the dead? Such dimension—to seem so volatile in one moment and so giving in the next.

To everything he touched, Jesus gave of his Light/Spirit, and in the few short years that people have heard most about him, he gave entirely of his life stream. This life stream was not only part of the Christ Consciousness, but it was also his own life stream. He had dedicated himself to the highest form

2. Levi, *The Aquarian Gospel of Jesus the Christ*. Marina del Rey, California: DeVorss & Co., 1964.

of Light in this creation that, to our knowledge, can ever be manifested or that ever will be.

It's interesting to remember the times Jesus walked along the roadway. I don't think many people consider the idea of a man who can walk along a road and get dusty feet yet be a God, a God in manifestation. Interestingly enough, those with him seemed to get very dirty along the road, while he seemed only to get dusty. Jesus demonstrated the Spirit by being able to move back from himself the things that he did not need.

We walk along the "roadway" of our lives and often get pretty dirty, picking up what is around us. But here was a man who so loved that nothing was above or below his consciousness. Jesus would wash his disciples' feet. He would feed them. When they were all asleep, he would wrap their robes around them to keep them warm. He worked with the people who needed the work.

Many times, religious groups came after Jesus to capture and detain him, but so many times were they thwarted that this also became a miracle. They would reach out for him and find he wasn't there. If he wanted to be surrounded and incarcerated, he had the consciousness to accept that, and if he didn't want that, nothing could harm him.

Jesus traveled all over the known world at that time. Some of those who were called forth as disciples traveled with him long before they were disciples assisting him in his open ministry in what we call the Holy Land (which is, indeed, a holy land because it has a vortex of energy that comes up through the earth).

There are so many things that can be told of that thirty-three-year period when this man went through more torment and agony than most people can ever imagine. Jesus' initiations into the various aspects of his ministry before he started ministering were beautiful to behold. Unless you can understand and see what was being brought forward, you will not know his way; only those who have eyes to see and ears to hear can know of the Light in its ministry.

With few exceptions, those who are part of the earth form will not know of this ministry through the Christ Consciousness. They will know of it when they are in another dimension. When they are taught in that dimension, the agony of their consciousnesses will be to look back on this planet and see where they could have grown so much more rapidly here in this consciousness because here on this physical level, we have such tremendous freedom. When we step into another kind of consciousness, we are restricted much more by certain laws; only on this planet do we have such freedom.

It's interesting to look back in time and see a man walking down the road at dusk. The company of Jesus sometimes got very hungry. They didn't have anyone to carry food for them, and they appeared to be at the mercy of the elements. But they really weren't because throughout the land where the ministry was taking place, there were groups of what we might call Light workers. They belonged to various sects, among which were the Essenes and the Nazarenes. As Jesus and his company went into these areas, everything would be taken care of for them. This was such a tremendous work and was laid down in such an ordered fashion that you might think it would have taken a general with a large staff to have set it up. Yet, in a moment of consciousness, these things were brought forward—because always and forever, wherever Jesus went, the Light moved ahead of him and the way was prepared for what he was to do.

When Jesus entered onto the planet as a baby, his birth was a phenomenon. Nothing else at the time was quite so phenomenal as when this baby was brought forward, and many people saw the ministry of angels coming forth.

Needless to say, the years before Jesus' open ministry were ones of intense study that very few people know about. He traveled under various names, and one was Joseph, or Joshua. If you could see the registers of the various mystery schools around the world, you would see the name Joseph/Joshua and the company he traveled with registered there. He was initiated into many mystery schools when he went into Persia and Egypt, and he even went into China.

When you stop to think about this man, he was, indeed, a world traveler. We could also say that he was a mystical traveler because wherever he went, the Christ Light went with him. He was overshadowed just about the age of thirty with the office of the Christ, and this was only after he had fulfilled all that was set before him to do—*all*. From the moment of his first breath, he was being educated to manifest the Christ action, to become the Christ for the planet, a God incarnate.

It's such a fantastic thing to have this type of action take place that we may not consciously realize what it is. The same air that was breathed by this great man, and others since, is still being breathed by each one of us; we are part, in more ways than you can imagine, of this particular action of the Light as it comes across the planet. We can refer to the Light as the "Christ Light," but we can also refer to it as being a universal energy source that comes from the supreme God—and this covers every race, religion, creed, and so on. It's all part of the divine action that is being brought forward.

Once Jesus was with sheep in a field when one got lost, and he went to find it. His parable of the lost sheep was not just a parable, you see; it was taken from his personal experience. Of course, when he found this lost sheep, he brought it back. Later, he brought forth the parable to show that not one Soul will be lost, not even the little "sheep" who doesn't know what's going on and who gets lost in the thickets of our civilization. A worker of Light will search this one out and bring it back to the fold.

There have been many Christs on the planet, but only a few have been able to manifest the Christ Consciousness in its highest glory and its highest manifestation. To be initiated into something is one action, but to manifest the initiation is another action. Many are called, but few choose back. You may be chosen to represent the Light, but you must also choose in return because the opportunity to manifest the Christ Light is never given to you but that you say, "Lord, I am ready. Here I am." Then the Light comes to you.

By presenting yourself in a position of acceptance, you go toward the Light. As this Light enters into your life, it can change you. It can lift you and purify you. I haven't seen anything yet that could not be done through this Light. We're all part of this focus, and as we continually bring forth our greater and greater Light, we are, indeed, doing it the way Jesus taught—not the way he saw so many doing it when he said, "Father, forgive them; for they know not what they do."[3] Jesus was also seeing ahead to the time when the teachings of the Christ would be perverted and corrupted through the hundreds of years after his death.

Together, the many dispensations over time can be looked at as a door through which we go. Jesus the Christ can be seen as the door's top hinge. There are other hinges on this door, and they are all manifestations of the unfolding Christ action. Still, we have to remember that no matter how many hinges there are on the door, we as individuals need to place our key (our consciousness) in the lock and make the necessary effort to turn the key and push open the door.

So many teachings have been brought forward about the actions of Light that 99 percent of the time we walk around in a quagmire, listening to all the different points of view and the different directions. We're hearing the same cry that was heard two thousand years ago. There were many different points of view then, too, because the people at that time were expecting a Messiah. Have you ever wondered what they looked forward to? The Pharisees thought he was going to come and fulfill the law. The Sadducees thought he was going

3. Luke 23:34 (Revised Standard Version)

to come and denounce the Pharisees. The Pharisees were upset because the scribes were recording all this. And the Nazarenes and Essenes thought none of them saw the truth as it really was.

Caiaphas was the high priest of the Jewish Sanhedrin, and every time a new Messiah appeared, he would say, "Let him go. He'll destroy himself pretty fast." Caiaphas would wait long enough, and the proposed Messiah would, indeed, discredit himself in many ways. He'd say things he couldn't back up or promise things that couldn't be fulfilled.

Then along came Jesus, who didn't really promise anything and didn't openly claim much. All he did was talk to people in the consciousness they were in. Yet many people missed what he was saying to them. So even though he was a master reigning in his glory two thousand years ago, he didn't reach everybody who was there—but only because everybody was not ready to work in a higher consciousness.

Even today, not everyone is ready to work in a higher consciousness. As nice as it would be to say, "Let's all go; we have the place prepared," the conscious part of us will often stand in our way. So our work, if we accept it, is to bring our consciousness into the higher understanding, into experiencing and knowing the Christ within.

2

Christ—The Self of Man

Jesus often referred to himself as the Son of man. When asked what he meant by that, he answered, "I am the self of man, the self of all humankind, the great inner knowing. This is what I am." When thought of this way, it can make more sense. The self of man is the Christ that is in every person, each one. Jesus manifested it to such a high degree of glory that he became that which is the Light.

Perhaps many of us have asked Jesus Christ for salvation. Yet if Jesus is the self of man and each of us is part of that self, then each of us is our own step toward salvation. We are our own doctrine. We are our own covenant. We are the temple of God. So we have a great responsibility. At the same time, we can't get stuck in a "holier-than-thou" attitude or in the opposite attitude of belittling ourselves.

A young man once called me and said, "I'm wasted, just wasted." As I am when anyone starts this with me, I was very quiet because if he had asked me what I thought, I'd probably have had to agree with him, since that was the consciousness he was expressing. But he had the wit to ask, "How do I stop this?" Then it became easy for him to ask how to change and grow.

I answered, "My young friend, if you were Jesus Christ returned today, what would you do?" Then he started solving his problem because he started looking at it through the eyes of the master.

Let's look at the idea of how you can look at things through the eyes of the master. By using your creative consciousness, you can bring forth the self that is you in the Christ Consciousness. To do this, you can start with generating within yourself the feeling of love for all humankind, a loving for everything on the planet. This doesn't mean that you have to go out and protect everything, and it doesn't mean that you have to be aware of every leaf that falls, but it does mean that you are very open.

You may sometimes feel as if you can't love your boss or your brother-in-law or someone else. Go back to the eyes of the master. Would the master love your boss? The answer is yes because the master loves you. It can be easy to move into this consciousness, but it's even more important to move deeper in your consciousness and tune in to the Inner Master, the inner expression of the Mystical Traveler. You can let yourself open and flow with the Holy Spirit. Ask for it within your consciousness. Ask for it with a prayer of welcome.

There is nothing quite so precious as your true self. The cosmic self or the Christ self is in contact with all knowledge and universal wisdom; even more important, it's in contact with God. Through your true self, you can rise so high that you may even seem large physically. You can lift yourself so dynamically that you may give the appearance of filling a room with your presence.

At the same time, you will know that you can't inflict yourself on any other Christ Consciousness. As you look at people, you can see their beauty and their love; you can see their Light. You can adore them for the Christ they are and can assist them, if it's for their highest good, in lifting into all consciousnesses that are theirs.

God didn't put you on this planet to be a beggar. God put you here and said, "You are the prince of the throne and an heir to all powers, principalities, and kingdoms. I will give you the Light. I will sustain you forever, and all you have to do is come back to me." Jesus also said, "Strait is the gate, and narrow is the way, which leadeth unto life, and few there be that find it."[1] God has made the promise; to enter into the fullness of that promise, you open to the Christ within you, which will guide you along the narrow way into greater spiritual awareness.

Your Christ Consciousness will eventually bring you into a position where you can enter into awareness of your true self, into your own movement of spiritual inner awareness. It will bring you to the point at which you become the messiah, the promised one. You become the alpha and the omega, from everlasting to everlasting—because you already are.

To me, that is the greatest heritage of the Christ Mass, or Christmas, as we celebrate it. We're actually celebrating our own birth. We're celebrating our own resurrection. We're celebrating triumphantly our own movement back into our true self or Christ Consciousness. In fact, many of us are just rushing into it, arms and heart wide open, full of love, and knowing that not one thing is coming our way that we can't handle.

1. Matthew 7:14 (King James Version)

The word *Christmas* is actually the words *Christ Mass*, which mean the worshiping of the Christ within each one of us and the partaking of that Spirit. We reach inward to the Christ and worship—not the person, but the God, the God of our hearts, the God of each one of us. At the time of the Christ Mass, it's almost as if the angels are touching very near to the hearts of men and women, especially those who are open to the eternal message of love, understanding, faith, hope, and charity.

The story of the Christ is one of universal symbolism that says that each one of us is the Anointed One, the Christ, the Messiah. If you update this story in your mind and bring it in as new—right now—you might very well discover something going on inside you that is the moving of your spiritual inner awareness. Some are more spiritually aware than others, but on whatever level you find yourself, that will be the level on which you approach the Father, the level on which you approach the Christ, and therein will you worship and pay homage.

Jesus the Christ spoke some simple truths, and as we tune in to and partake of the inner Light, we know that all things are eternal and that there is a season and a time for all things. We know that when our time is full upon us, we do give birth to the Christ within. It's there. Many times the seed is there in barren or scorched soil, but it is still there. It will always be there, just waiting for us to scratch below the surface of our consciousness and bring the determination of who we are to bear upon this seed of greatness and usher it forward.

Jesus' life symbolizes the birth of Christ within each person. We've probably all been sorely taxed in one way or another in our travels across this planet. I'm sure we've all had trials and tribulations and have cried out, "Oh Lord, Lord, how much longer?" Maybe we didn't hear anything, so we knew it had to be a little longer. Then we may have turned to our fellow men and women and asked, "How much longer?" Then we knew it still had to be a little longer because we heard nothing.

The Travelers come forward to tell you of the other realms of consciousness and to say, "We can all go, and we can go now. But to go high, we must be free of all the chains that bind and confine us here on the planet." So we joyfully unshackle ourselves and learn to use wisdom to step forward in those areas that are for our highest good.

You may have found that your highest good may sometimes be a little different from what you thought it should be. You may ask for the highest good; then something happens and you say, "That doesn't feel too good." Yet later on, you may look back and say, "I'm so glad I went through that. That taught me a tremendous lesson. A valuable experience came forward."

As you go through your lessons, remember that you cannot destroy the true self. No matter what you do, it cannot be destroyed. The negative power cannot destroy this self. It can make the body pretty miserable, but when that body is miserable, remember that you can move away from it into a higher consciousness.

For example, I once met a woman, and I looked at her and said, "My, the pain in your body is fantastic."

She asked, "How did you know this?"

I answered, "Because of many reasons, and let's let it go at that. But tell me, how do you live within that body?"

"I don't," she said. "I live in my higher self. I know there's pain in the body; there's cancer all through it. I know this body does things other people can't appreciate. I know it's only a burden on them, but it doesn't burden me. I keep lifting higher and higher."

If you were to look at this woman, you'd probably think, "What an angel." You'd never think there was anything wrong in her body. She was manifesting the higher consciousness and was getting very close to finding the true self.

We can never be parted from the true self. As we resolve to remove each block, reaching further and further into this higher consciousness, we let our hearts sing joyfully, for unto us this day is given our birth. We are born anew into our own unfoldment, into the spiritual Light.

Let's not be too concerned with the little physical problems we have. Maybe we sometimes do have one beer too many, eat too much candy, or overindulge in other areas, but let's not hold these things against ourselves. If someone doesn't see eye to eye with us, that's fine because it gives us a chance to see that person's point of view, and when we see that point of view, we expand our consciousness even more. As we lift higher and higher and we travel further and further through all the realms of Light, we will know we are masters, we are the Light, we are of Spirit, we are gods in manifestation.

So rejoice—because the knowledge is yours. And now you must manifest it, understand it, and know that you know, for you are, indeed, holy. Everywhere you go is sacred ground, every person you touch to is a sacred person, and each consciousness is to be respected. All the hurts, the heartaches, and the sorrows can be turned over to the Inner Master, and there they will be dissolved through the Holy Spirit.

If things in the past have seemed rough for you, it may be that the barriers to your true self were being stripped away. Once you see the Soul, once you can glimpse that self within you in all its majesty and glory—oh, my friend, nothing the world can give you is going to mean too much from that point on. Someone may give you a new house, a Cadillac, furs, jewelry, a lot of money—whatever—and you'll say, "Yes, all right, okay. Now let's get going. I want to get back to the self." It will be like a little child giving an adult a mud pie. You'll say, "Yes, yes, very nice. Now let's go on." That's the way these material things may look to you.

But still, we're in the flesh, and this is where we're going to work out and balance much of our karma. We'll work out a good percentage of it here physically, and the rest of it will be worked out while the body is sleeping.

If you don't get caught up in the physical world, you can feel yourself lifting. But don't try to escape the world; don't do anything to escape it. So many people now are running so fast just to get away from themselves, yet are having to come back to the true self. We have to come back to it in a natural, orderly way. We have to come back and say, "Here I am, Lord, the co-heir to the throne and the prince of all time."

Just realize for a moment that you *are* the heir. Nothing can be denied you. Of course, you have to work off the things you've earned from your past actions, but when you've worked these off, you can find that you may order the universes of Light and that they bow down to you. The angels of the highest realms of Light minister to you when you realize you are Christed, when you realize your true self is divine and eternal, from everlasting to everlasting.

It's so beautiful that the Light brings people together from every level of society, from all races and all religions. The Light doesn't care from which racial heritage you descend, and it doesn't care if you're a banker, a robber, a housewife, or a dentist. It doesn't care. It just wants to join you in worshiping your own divine self. So when you ask for the Light to move in with you, it does—so joyfully that you can be lifted.

The Light also knows that its loyalty is always to the supreme God, to that One who must remain nameless. Consciously, we may sometimes say, "Maybe my loyalty is to my bank book or my job." While we get hung up on those things, the Light is busy showing us that we must continue toward God.

When the Traveler says, "Come, let's go to this place that has been prepared," we can then lay aside the material things, which will perish, and step into the spiritual realms and be with that which never perishes. We can step from the consciousness we call the physical into what we call the spiritual, where we know that nothing can separate us, that nothing can stand in our way, and that we can place the Light wherever we are.

It is our destinies this time on the planet to lift the consciousness of the world and actually prepare it for the golden age that is now approaching. Those of us in MSIA are that golden bridge from the consciousness of yesterday to the consciousness of tomorrow. We'll walk back and forth on that bridge many times, taking the Light to the people of yesterday and walking with them across that golden bridge of promise to the consciousness of tomorrow. We'll show them the way and be Light bearers, because the spiritual Light is seen with unseeing eyes and the spiritual Sound is heard with unhearing ears.

3

Christ Consciousness—Day by Day

Each of us has probably asked many times, "How do I get to God?" You get there by overcoming your conscious self in the mind and stepping into your Christ Consciousness, which is the Soul, your true self.

The true self can be recognized by the attributes of love, charity, and wisdom. Most of us find it easy to love when we get something we want, but can we still love when we don't get what we want? Can we assist other people without inflicting ourselves on them? Can we lovingly help them with something without taking the experience and their learnings away from them?

One of the biggest things I have to work with in my consciousness is seeing people manifesting so much beautiful Light and then wanting to move in and try to make everything perfect. That would be easy to do. It's harder to stand back and love and let people go through their experiences, but that's what I do because I love them and want them to get the experiences that will help them to grow into an even greater awareness of God.

Your agony is my agony because I sense it so intently with you, and the love you give me is a love that sustains me and assists me in giving love back to you. There's an old saying through the line of Mystical Travelers: "If you love the master, he's always with you. If you don't love the master, he's always with you, but you might not know it." It's the same thing with the Christ Consciousness. When we love it intently, it's with us, but even when we don't love it—even if we curse it—it's still with us, but we might not know it.

There is one truth that is repeatable: "You and I are one. I am always with you, as you are always with me." Knowing that, I never walk alone, and neither do you. When you falter a little, there will be a Light bearer there to steady you—not to take the step for you (because a Light bearer won't do that), but to steady you so you can take your next step.

As *Light* bearers, we support every action, no matter what it is. We can love each and every person, no matter who they are, what they say, or what they do. We look through the eyes of the master at all people, and with adoration we love them just as we love little children—because we are all children of God.

When we become one with the Christ Consciousness, we become the only begotten, one in the great Ocean of Love and Mercy. So, if you will, take love, charity, and wisdom to use wherever you go. Let people come to you to be lifted; they'll probably search you out. Give them the chance to come to you, and don't hold yourself aloof from them. You may tell them nothing about the Light, but by your being full of love, charity, and wisdom, they'll get the message.

You can go forward into this world, anointing, blessing, and lifting, maybe without even mentioning a word about the Light. Much of the action will be love, and much of it will be truth. You can see what's going on; nobody's fooling you. You know what is important to you and where you are going. If someone isn't doing what you are, that's okay. Whatever they do, you're with them. That doesn't necessarily mean that you're going to do what they do because, really, they are the only one who can breathe their air, digest their food, and make their blood flow. Whatever way they decide to do it is okay.

We also say to people that if there comes a time when what they're doing isn't working for them, then look for the truth and have the wit to change those things that aren't working and move to those things that are. If things work on Monday and not on Tuesday, be sure to drop them on Tuesday.

You are the messiah, but you must know it within your own Christ Consciousness before you can bring it forward and manifest it. When you listen to these truths with the "third ear," you can hear so much and your consciousness can become so much greater.

So we take a few moments and tune in to the Inner Master. Within that consciousness, we can rededicate ourselves to our oneness with God and resolve that we'll make each stumbling block that comes our way into a stepping-stone. On each stone that bruises us in our travels, we'll shed the spirit of life and Light and, if necessary, anoint each stone with our blood.

We also bring forth love, charity, and wisdom, so that we may know we are on the path of Light and move through all levels of consciousness. We resolve to say a good word even after we have said bad words, to see something beautiful within each person, movement, and situation. The angels of Light are attending us. The masters of the spiritual hierarchy are blessing us as we spiritually partake of the Christ Mass and open ourselves into the higher dimensions. The Lord Jesus said, "Lo, I am with you always, to the close of the age,"[1] and we know the truth of that statement. We know that the Spirit within each of us is one and that we can never be separated.

Within this oneness, each person has many levels of consciousness, three major ones being the lower self or basic self (which has responsibility for bodily functions and maintains the psychic centers of the body), the conscious self (the self of which we are aware in our day-to-day lives), and the high self (which acts as a person's spiritual guardian). Human beings speak from these different levels at different times, and Jesus exemplified this in many ways. He spoke from the level of the lower self as he cleansed the temple. He spoke from the level of the conscious self when he talked to people and discussed the parables. And he spoke from the level of the higher self when he said, "I am the way, and the truth, and the life; no one comes to the Father, but by me."[2]

Where is the Father found? How do we find eternal life? The Bible sometimes does not give us specific answers to our questions, but you must understand that the Bible is coded to protect the great knowledge that is in it. Otherwise, people

1. Matthew 28:20 (Revised Standard Version)
2. John 14:6 (Revised Standard Version)

who are not initiated into the mysteries of the inner Light could corrupt it and use it to abuse, hurt, and control.

By "doing it for you," people can gain control over you, making you a spiritual cripple and holding you in bondage to them. They may do this inadvertently, thinking they are assisting you by telling you what to do and making your decisions for you. But they are really binding you (not releasing you) by doing this.

A person may call my name, and I listen and often answer, "You must do that yourself. You must make that decision. But make it wisely because, as a creator, you're going to be bound by that choice."

The person may say, "Yes, I realize that, and I'll make good choices. It's okay. I know I'll have to live with the results of my choices." They may consider their choices carefully, or they may make haphazard decisions or say, "I'll decide later."

One day, for example, I had the chance to talk to a beautiful friend of mine I hadn't seen physically for well over a year. He told me about some difficulties he was having and asked, "What am I going to do?"

I said, "Handle it now."

"No, no," he said. "I'll handle it later."

"Look," I told him, "this thing you're in now is one of your 'laters.'"

"How do you know?" he asked.

"How do you know it's *not?*"

"Because I say so," he said.

I said, "Then I have answered all I can answer for you and have done all I can do for you."

Jesus helped everybody but the fools, and he let the fools go their own way. You may ask and ask and ask—and while you are asking, you are getting the answers, but you may be so busy thinking of the next question that you may miss the answers.

Sometimes you ask and get no answer, and you may get disturbed and think, "I've been forsaken and let down." Did you ever stop to think that maybe there was no answer at that time? It just might be that you were not to do anything, that you were to hold firm to the Light that you are, that you were to just take that next breath and quiet the lower self.

When you get hurt or experience butterflies in the stomach, anxieties, and apprehensions, you may ask, "Why me? Why me?" The answer may be, "Because you're handy." But if you don't like a situation, you can get out of it; you have a right to do that. There are a lot of ways to get out of something, and the best way can often be to sit down and very quietly say, "Father, here I am. I don't know too much. Sometimes I like to think I do, but I'm not too smart, even though I can talk big. But maybe, just once, will you extend to me the graciousness of helping?"

That small voice wherein the Inner Master speaks to you may very well say, "My Beloved, it is just a while longer that you are here. Can you not endure all things to find the kingdom of heaven?"

So you may say, "Yes, Lord, I can. But is that going to be by tomorrow?"

It might be terrible to think you have to die to "collect," but that's not the message Jesus the Christ brought forward. He preached of a heaven right now. He preached of the Light right now. He said, in essence, "It's here. If you pray, believing your prayer will be answered, it is done."[3] Prayer that comes out as a control pattern will rarely bring you what you really want. But prayer that is a greater Light attunement and that is reaching to the Christ Consciousness within will bring to you those things that are for your highest good.

Whether we reside in this physical body or outside of it, life is eternal. That's another thing the master Jesus said: "If you believe in me, you shall have eternal life."[4] He was not referring to himself as Jesus the man, but as Jesus the consciousness of the Christ. If you believe in a man, you may go down into your own purgatory, into the hell of your own making. Then you drop lower than the lower self and express in that way. On that level, all that seems to get done is, "Feed me. Make sure my stomach is full. Make sure I have a place to sleep." But Jesus said that the Son of man has no place to lay his head.[5]

It is a paradox that we must give up everything to have everything. We must sacrifice all things to receive all things. You may say, "Lord, I want to know. I want to have enlightenment."

3. Matthew 21:22
4. John 3:15
5. Luke 9:58

So Spirit says, "What will you exchange for this? Will you give up all things? Will you pick up your cross and follow me?"

"No, no," you may say, "I don't want to do that. But I will go to church on Sunday if that's all that's asked. I don't want to make it every week, though, because some Sundays I like to go fishing, do things with my family, or play golf. So if I can have it on my terms, Lord, I'll take it. Okay, I'm ready."

Then it may seem as if nothing happens. But it may be that you just aren't seeing the enlightenment that is taking place or hearing the inner voice that is saying to you, "That way isn't going to work. It will not bring you what you really want."

So then you may go to a different teacher and be introduced to new ideas. You may say, "I will pray fervently night and day, saying the name of the Lord. How's that?" If you don't hear anything, you may think, "Maybe he's just waiting." So you pray and pray and pray. It may become rather mechanical, but you still pray. Then one day, perhaps you get in trouble, and out of the very depths of your beingness you cry out, "Help!" Then in the door walks your answer, and you know it's your answer because the problems are clearing up, and things in general are getting clearer. Who you are comes into focus. How to handle things becomes clearer. You learn to keep your mouth shut, which can also clear up a lot of things.

God knows that, ultimately, all things will come into alignment as part of your understanding. When you realize that all things are added to you according to your understanding, it's much easier for you to flow through this life. You may say, "I understand, I understand. Reveal something to me." So you are given a secret, which you tell to the first person you see on the street: "Guess what I know!" Then the information may be shut off to you, and you can't understand this.

When you understand the nature of your beingness, you have the key to all creation, and the key is this: when we pray fervently from deep within the conscious self (where we are now), we charge our lower self with this prayer, and it will release energy up into the high self. The high self will then send the energy back down into the lower self, until the lower self is so charged with energy that it forces the energy back up into the conscious self. With this spiritualized energy, our consciousness rises. That's why we don't have to go anywhere except within.

But sometimes we ask, "Where is 'within'? If the kingdom of heaven is within, where is that?" It is a consciousness, not necessarily a physiological location. We go past the superficial things and into our consciousness. We learn to close our eyes to those things that will distract or corrupt us, that will prevent us from reaching into the high self. There are many people on this planet who have reached into their high selves, and they all have the same message: "I am the way, the truth, and the light. I am that I am."

I think we've all found out the meaning behind the old statement, "The path is straight and narrow." We have all been sorely tempted to stray into things of the lower self. But when we educate this lower consciousness and bring it into alignment and fulfillment, we have unified all our levels of consciousness, and all things in all existences will bow down. Because it will be our own Christ Mass at which we'll be feasting, it will be a beautiful day. We can rejoice in it.

Lest you be confused by the things of this physical world, close your eyelids that you may see, and close your ears that you may hear. You must reach into a higher level than where you are now. Young children do this automatically. They hear, they see, they are. And they fuss and squirm when you force the physical world on them because they're not yet prepared to handle it.

Do you want to know how great you are? Look at how you handle the physical world. This is a rough place in which to work. It's not enough just to breathe the air; you also have to get through all the illusions that are here.

Still, there is a reality on this planet, and that reality is your Soul. That is what makes all things real and all things new. So you come into the New Jerusalem of your own consciousness, where all things are made new. You become the sacrifice of the Father. What does it profit you to gain the physical world and lose (remain unaware of) your Soul? What good does it really do you when you reach out into the physical world for that man or that woman and discover they're out with someone else? What good does it do you to have a broken heart? When you reach into the treasures of heaven, all things are brought forward to you in a right and proper way through the Father.

Jesus said, "No one can come to me unless the Father who sent me draws him."[6] This makes all things right and proper;

6. John 6:44 (Revised Standard Version)

this makes everything new. Each moment and each breath are new. Lest you get caught in yesterday, your work is to keep yourself conscious in the present. When you find yourself drifting off in your thoughts, this is telling you, "Your work is cut out for you. You are not handling *right now*. How can you handle greater things when you can't handle the lesser things?"

So we're continually coming back to this moment. We're continually watching the emotions, and when our emotions overwhelm us, we say, "Satan, get thou behind me. Do not corrupt me, but get in your proper place and allow me to do the work of the Father." When we do the Father's work, we do everything at a higher level. When we do human work, we do things in a physical way, and those physical things will corrupt, decay, and pass away.

Jesus as the Christ, speaking to each one of us, said, "Come, follow me. I have a place prepared for you." Though you might not be there now, you will be able to be there sometime. The Cosmic Christ comes forward at this time in the consciousness of Light and says, "Come, follow me. We have a place prepared for you that is yours *now*. We will teach you to see beyond the physical and show you the higher realms."

People rarely do this by themselves. They must be shown the key and patiently assisted in lifting their consciousness. And remember, if you can be lifted by someone else, you can be thrown down. Lest anyone throw you down, *lift yourself*. When you do, you'll find that people will stand tall with you. They'll stand serene with you. Then if you start to fall, you'll find that they're there for you to lean on temporarily, but they won't do it for you. When you start to waver within yourself, it's nice to be able to turn to another Light bearer and say, "What do you see that can help me?" The greatest thing that can be said to you is, "You are the Light. Move into your Father in heaven, and see through the eyes of the master what is happening."

We are all masters on one level of consciousness or another. To know that you are the master is one of the greatest gifts that can be bestowed upon you. Then the gates of hell cannot prevail against you. Nothing can harm you except that the Father in your heaven allows it—and then it will be for the glory of all humankind that you take upon yourself a burden to show other people that it can be handled, that it can be done. You can continually unfold in this eternal knowledge that you are the master.

4

Going Home

Christmas means many different things to people and brings forward many levels of expression. We have often heard one level in songs and stories, the idea that "I want to be home for Christmas." It's a phrase that seems to mean a great deal to many of us. So as I was contemplating this idea a while ago, I wondered what "home" means to all the beautiful Souls who gather together to celebrate the Christ Mass. I wondered what message the idea of "home" might bring to them, what message might awaken them another step so they could evolve even higher.

I wondered, "Where is our home, to which we all want to go? Where does it exist?" I considered the physical structure that is my house, and I thought, "Yes, that is a form of home." I considered the place where my parents used to live, and I thought, "Yes, that's also a form of home." Then I thought of where my father lived after my mother dropped the physical body, and that was a form of home, too. Yet none of these things is really Home.

The year my mother passed away, she was visiting with me and said, "I want to be home for Christmas this year."

I said, "You will be. There's no question about that."

She asked, "Do you really think so?"

"Yes," I said. "There is no question that you will be *home for Christmas*." Then that spring when she left the body, she found that she was Home, and I was so joyful to realize that she was experiencing that fulfillment of truly being Home.

The Christ Mass of Home is in each person's heart. Where there is love, there we have found Home. If we are residing in the Christ, then we are Home. It's reality to reside within the Christ; it's unreality, if not impossibility, to do otherwise. When Jesus came forward and said that he had no place to lay his head,[1] he was really implying that the Christ resides everywhere and that that consciousness never really lays down its head. This is the part of us that is eternally awake and that lives eternally.

Some people are waiting fervently for the Christ to return. They're hoping and praying for him to return, not realizing that he may never have left. It's interesting: some people are praying he'll come, yet others are scared he will. Many people feel they're probably going to hell, so they feel that the return of the Christ might be a great calamity to them. Some would like to go to heaven, but in their Soul-searching they say, "Well, I don't think I'm quite prepared. So if you don't mind, Lord, don't come just yet. But do keep coming this way."

People who say this have not really studied the scripture; if they had, they would know that Christ said that he is always with us, even unto the end.[2] Then has he ever left, or does the

1. Luke 9:58
2. Matthew 28:20 (King James Version)

Christ resides all the time with us? The only thing we have to do is awaken to our own Christhood, to that level of consciousness within. When we're there, we are Home. Everything else is then secure, and there is nowhere else to go. It is from that position of Christ Consciousness that we salute the Christ in every being walking the planet.

I once saw something very interesting while looking at the spiritual records. There was a young child sitting on a chair with a cloth or blanket draped over his lap to keep his body warm. The child appeared healthy and happy; his eyes were sparkling and glowing. The mother of the child came along and picked him up, and, as the blanket fell away, I could see that there were no legs on the body. There was just a torso with no legs. But that little child put his hands up on his mother's face, and with the love he had and the love she had, they were Home.

This is also one of the many ways that the Christ manifests itself eternally to each one of us. When we look into each other's eyes, bypassing the personality and the idiosyncrasies, we are looking into the windows of the Soul. When we move into our own Christ center, we can gaze into the Christ within the other person, and we find that we can look at another without feeling anything but this spiritual love. Then we partake again of the Christ within and without.

There is nothing quite so valuable as people because of the divine spark that is within each one. If you try to place anything above people, you have entered into an illusion. When a child cries and that causes you disturbance, you should certainly check your own levels because beyond that child's emotional expression resides the Christ. When someone appears to have a physical disability or handicap and you are disturbed by it, look beyond that expression to the Christ that resides within. If someone is emotionally upset, look beyond that upset to the Christ within. It's there.

It's important to remember that we have all cried out to the Father. Many say, "I'm ready, Father. Take me Home… but do it my way." I believe they are really saying, "Lord, show me the way, and I'll make it my way. If it can't adapt to me, I'll adapt to it." When we say that, we are residing within the strength, the wisdom, and the love of the Christ Consciousness.

The Aquarian Gospel recounts Jesus' birth and says that "three persons clad in snow-white robes came in and stood before the child and said, All strength, all wisdom and all love be yours, Immanuel."[3] When they said this, they were identifying the attributes of the Christ Consciousness. You see, in the Christ we have all strength, but strength without wisdom is abuse, and wisdom without love to help us express it becomes arrogance.

When we have entered into strength, wisdom, and love and have balanced these, we will not use them to hurt people or to say, "I have found the way and you haven't." Instead, once again, we rediscover the idea of, "Father, you are in me, and I am in you. We need each other. But even more important, we *are* each other." If we are one with the Father, then we are also one with each one of our brothers and sisters everywhere.

1. Levi, The Aquarian Gospel (3:6-7)

We're approaching a golden age. People say, "That's wonderful! No more wars. Everything's going to be fine." My point of view is that it may not be *that* golden. The wars might be a little more "enjoyable," though. There might not be quite as much mayhem, but there are still going to be some difficulties on this level because this level is designed for that. But we can look forward to the Light sweeping onto the planet more and more each year.

Many psychics have said that we will be seeing more evil on the planet than ever before, but I'd like to say that there will also be more Light on the planet than ever before. When the Light comes with its tremendous power, the negativity cannot stay; it must be stirred up and thrown out. So as the Light manifests, we may see much of humanity's inhumanity. But we should thank God for this action of the Light, which brings up and out the imbalance that cannot stay in the presence of the Holy Spirit.

You may sit and hold the Light for people in a room, just *being* the Light and manifesting it through your presence. Then when people go out, turmoil may arise as their lives get cleaned up—because this Light will go with them into their homes and families. You may say, "I don't know whether the Light is any good at all. Look at the things that appear to be going wrong. Things seem worse. Look at what it's doing. Look at all the trouble and turmoil." This is because the Light throws the negativity up and cleans it out. It brings everything into balance. It must; otherwise, it's masquerading.

The Light will not masquerade anywhere. If you're out of balance, you cannot stay in the presence of the Light. If you say, "This is it; I've reached it; nothing is higher than this," then you're not working in the Light, and you may be working with sham. Many, many times the Light brings discontent so you'll get up and get going. If you become too content and placid, you may not grow or do anything, and each person's destiny on this planet is to grow and to learn.

One reason you're here is to experience—not to be pigeon-holed or labeled a "this" or a "that." You move through many expressions, but you don't get boxed in by the lessons you're here to learn. You experience them and learn from them. You say, "Thank you, Lord, for that opportunity," and you move on.

As you move on, you can then face and accept yourself in any position in your consciousness, and many initiations can be brought your way. As these initiations are brought to you, you must be found worthy inside your spirit personality to accept them. It can be a sad day for you if you are presented with an initiation and then find you aren't capable of handling it.

So, as you are preparing yourself for future initiations, remember that you are the Light and that this Light can be passed to others through your consciousness. If you can allow people to express the Light their own way, to fulfill their own destiny, and to walk the path to the drummer they hear, then you have, in essence, done the same thing God does—allowed them the freedom of their own expression. Freedom of expression also means responsibility of beingness. When we express, we are responsible for that expression. So we might want to make sure our expressions are beautiful and "Lightful."

I'd like to share with you a beautiful expression of "Light verse" written by a friend of mine:

I stood in the glow of our Christmas tree,
Its essence reaching out to me.
Entranced in its spell I felt so very well,
Watching the many colored lights
Ascending into one of white,
Which stood serenely perched atop the tree
And radiated down to me
A multicolored harmony.
Behind the Christmas trees and twinkling gleam,
Behind laughing faces and giving gifts,
Behind well wishes and "deck the halls,"
Behind Christmas,
There is a magic to it all.
Somehow within each year
Comes this one day to all so dear
That men everywhere lay down their fear
To be full of love and full of good cheer.
What is this feeling that comes and goes,
That each of us feels and few of us know,
That fills the heart and thrills the Soul,
That takes all the pieces and makes them whole?
There's a magic in Christmas, a secret surprise,
Hidden within us until we finally realize
That it is our own birth in total liberation
That is the reason for all the celebration.
That is the real magic of the Christ Mass,
A magic through which we all shall pass,
To return to our true selves and the Kingdom within,
Saying, "Peace on earth and God's will to all men."

So, once again, we come into a sense of oneness, greater than we've ever had before. We express more joy, more Light, and more love than ever before. We open our hearts to that one called the Christ. You can make him your personal savior; you can make the Christ of your own heart your personal savior. It will all work—if you work it. There are no barriers, no restrictions on universal spiritual love. There is only oneness and beingness. There is only God.

In the inner realms of Light, it is always day because it is always Light. And in this beautiful day, all things are made eternally new. We may say, "Father, I come to do thy will. Thy law is written in my heart. And when I stray from the path of thy guidance, then I will return eternally and fulfill again the Christ Consciousness that is my heritage."

5

Living the Christ Consciousness

e are not alone on this planet; we never have been. Eternally, there have been Light bearers who bring forward all things new. Now all things are made new as we make them new. As this Light of the Holy Spirit is brought forward to us, we say, "O God, we receive of your Light and your Love. Lest we do not fulfill our eternal vow, we ask again to be strengthened in letting this Light of Father-Mother God flow through all levels where we are right now and enter deep within each level of our consciousness. We come again, Father, and we do sacrifice all things physical. We will take care of all things physical, but we will not let them abuse us. We are the life and the truth and the way. We are eternal. Our progression is never-ending. We can only grow."

It is a great message, a beautiful message, which says that we can only go forward, we can only go up. We can show other people and let them walk with us, but we won't lean on them. Nor will we allow them to lean on us for very long—only long enough to let them steady themselves and to show them their own Light so they'll find their own way.

People strive to reach into the Christ Consciousness, into heaven. We can have heaven here on Earth by just going in and saying, "Father, here I am. I receive. I don't question because I might not know what's going on. But by my faith you can give to me, and by my works you will know my understanding. My belief is that I also am the Christ, that I also am love, faith, hope, and charity." As each new day comes to us, we say, "Father, it's a good day because it's yours, and it's going to be a fulfilling day because it's mine. We'll walk together and make all things new."

You are a bearer of the Light. The Light of the Christ, the inner Light, is eternal. It won't go out; it will only go up. Your job is cut out for you: it is to put the Light around the world, to live each moment in the Light, and to *be* the Light. You are the Light. I know your Light. I know your beauty. I know the Soul. I endeavor to show you that wisdom so that you, too, can know it—not to throw you out of balance with yourself, but to bring you into balance.

You hunger and thirst only when you have not reached into the depths of your own Light, which springs forth eternally. It's difficult to dip into the spring of someone else's consciousness of Light in the physical world and find fulfillment. Your fulfillment comes from within you. Many people can hold your hand while you strive and while you seek help. Some may try to do it for you, and in their unknowing love, they may "damn" you each step of the way by taking away your experiences and your opportunities to learn. If you can realize that you are the Light of the world and that through you all things exist and come to pass, then other people can catch this vision. When they do, they may be able to know this about themselves, too, and to share that vision with others they meet, in an endless pattern of fulfillment.

We are all expressions of Spirit. The Soul is Spirit individualized, manifesting through the physical body on this plane. There is nothing so sacred, so enduring, and so lasting as the God in each person's heart. So fill your heart with the beingness of love, and let it flow like you have never let it flow before. Don't be afraid to be who you are. Don't be afraid of being criticized or condemned. You get criticized more when you hold back from expressing your divine attributes.

Every day, you will express more eternal love. Release past disturbances; let them go. Be thankful, be joyful for *now*, for in this now, you will know, once again, that you are the promised one. You will know that the Messiah is, indeed, on the planet, that he is bringing forward a greater dispensation, that he is moving the planet forward into a golden age, and that the visions of young men and women will be fulfilled in the years to come.

Realize that you are biblical scripture now being written and that centuries from now, the lives that are being enthroned in the spiritual records at this time will be the "Bible" of people who will say, "If I had lived in that time, if I could have partaken of that Christ Consciousness, then I, too, could have been saintly. I, too, could have expressed eternal love."

Now the prayer of our hearts reaches up once again as we say, "Father, here we are. We don't even know fully who you are, but we love you dearly. We're happy here, but we want to go Home. We want to live eternally within your divine consciousness."

We can do this every moment because as we move our spiritual inner awareness higher, we find ourselves entering into the gates of our own beingness, where there is great joy. When you think of joy, think of the letters: J-O-Y. For the first letter, think of Jesus. Put Jesus first in this joy. Give out the Christ love within you to the Christ love within Jesus, and make it one.

Then take the O in joy and let that stand for others. Think of Jesus first and others second—your family, your employer, your employees, people you see on the street. Let this Light radiate to them all. Your love for Jesus is love returned to you to be given to others.

And now the Y—yourself. Put Jesus first, others second, and yourself third. And for yourself, bring in all things. Take to yourself the joy of beingness. There's nothing quite so beautiful as Souls in harmony. There's nothing quite so beautiful as one mind, one emotion, one feeling, one Spirit—and that is the one of your true self, the Christ within you, the joyful beingness of the nameless One.

The
Disciples
of
Christ

1

The Disciples of Christ

Much has been written and said about Jesus the Christ, and many people have tried to interpret the action of the Christ. We tend to sit here, in this contemporary time, and say, "If I'd lived in that time, I wouldn't have been the one who crucified Jesus. I would have known better. What a stupid thing to do, to kill Jesus."

Yet *how would we recognize the Christ if he appeared tomorrow?* How would we know him? What would he have to say, and what would he have to do? Would he come in robes, sandals, and long hair? Would he walk on water? Would he come and feed the multitudes with a few fish?

Some people say that they are waiting for the Christ to return. How is he supposed to return? What is the preconceived idea of what will take place? Will he return in glory? If so, what kind of glory? The glory he had before? Remember, people crucified him last time. Many people did not recognize Jesus as the Christ. They did not recognize the Spirit as it flowed through him.

If the Christ returned today, those who would recognize him would know him in the same way that the disciples of

Jesus knew that he was the Christ. Those people who are aware of the Christ Light within themselves can recognize this Light in another. One time, Jesus asked his disciples, "Who do you say that I am?"

Simon Peter answered, "You are the Christ."

Jesus said, "Flesh and blood has not revealed this to you, but my Father who is in heaven."[1]

Jesus also said that "the kingdom of God is within you,"[2] so the Father, the Spirit, must be within each person. That Spirit that bore testimony to the Christ Spirit in Jesus was a lesser amount of the same consciousness of the Christ Spirit within Peter himself. The Light of the Christ is recognized by your own Christ Light within. It can't be recognized any other way. Everyone carries the Christ Light, but some are more aware of that Light and are able to recognize and manifest that Light to a greater extent. Jesus was manifesting the highest awareness pattern on the planet, the awareness of this Light.

Jesus' disciples were just people, as we are just people. They were very much attached to their own consciousnesses, their own patterns of behavior, and their own emotions, needs, and desires. The consciousness of each one could manifest in a negative way or a positive way. Power and energy can be used to destroy, or they can be used to create and build. For example, the power of criticism and faultfinding can also be used for praise and upliftment; critical judgment can be used to point out what is wrong or what is right in a situation.

1. Matthew 16:15-17 (Revised Standard Version)
2. Luke 17:21 (King James Version)

We are going to look at Jesus' disciples and the consciousness that each one manifested. The twelve stages of consciousness that are represented by the disciples are within each one of us, and at some time each person has portrayed each stage, each level. By understanding the attributes of each disciple, we can apply that understanding to ourselves, as we move more into expressing the higher consciousness in our everyday lives.

During the time of Jesus, the consciousness of each disciple was moved from the negative aspect to the positive aspect as Jesus awakened the Light in each one. As the Light flowed through each disciple, the things that were negative were reversed in polarity and became positive. We can change in the same way that they changed, by the same action of the Light of the Christ.

Jesus called forth these twelve men who were able to see the Christ action and the Spirit within him, and he placed these twelve around him as a large focal point of his expression throughout his ministry. They were chosen over quite a period of time. As they were chosen and came in, Jesus worked with each one personally, explaining the Light action and the manifestation of the Light. Each one was selected and trained, and then, as each new one came in, the others would also help with his training. They continually passed this information to each one as they built the brotherhood of mankind. The spiritual fellowship within that circle of Light was beautiful because they shared with each other, and each one lifted the consciousness of the others as they contributed their knowledge down the line.

Andrew

First, there was Andrew, who is thought of as the second apostle, although he was the first called. Jesus spoke to him and said, in essence, "I want you to come and hold the Light. I want you to come and work with me, be a Light bearer, become a fisher of men." (A "fisher of men," at that time, meant a spiritual person.) When Jesus spoke, the Light within him activated the Light within Andrew so that Andrew's spiritual eyes were opened.

Andrew was so filled with the Spirit that Jesus radiated through the Christ action that he went to his brother, Simon (who became Peter), and said, "I want you to meet a man who is probably the greatest man who will walk in this dispensation." And this Light, which had come through the Christ, went through our great friend Andrew to Peter and led Peter to the Christ to become the first apostle. The two brothers went to Jesus, and Jesus looked at Peter and said, "Come, follow me." Even though Andrew was the first called, he gave up this position to be second, and we equate the action of this consciousness of Andrew with humility.

If Christ came to us today and said, "Come, follow me," I wonder how many of us could say, "Just a minute; I want to get my brother or sister," and bring them forward and say, "You can be first, and I'll be second." We might tend to say, "I was called first. I'm first. I didn't decide it. *He* decided it." The Andrew consciousness is rather rare on the planet. Yet, to receive the Light, we have to have the Andrew consciousness. We have to be humble enough to recognize that there is a great force and to say, "When it calls, I hope I am able to recognize it and be brought forward into the action."

Humility is really a consciousness of acceptance. Jesus manifested this same consciousness when he washed the feet of his disciples. He humbled himself to the least position. There is a force who works with me, and he taught me a beautiful lesson one day when he said, "In God's kingdom there is nothing great or nothing low, but you must express all levels of consciousness when called upon."

Peter

Let me give you a thumbnail sketch of Peter. Sometimes it's hard to realize that the disciples were just men. Peter, for example, could be a real hellion. He liked to look around, and he held a lot of different jobs. You might say he was a roustabout; he was also a fisherman, a farmer, a bricklayer, a builder. He couldn't settle down and didn't have a very good foundation for his life. He had joined various organizations at that time. He didn't know what he wanted out of life; he was looking for *something*, and so this gave the appearance of his being a restless drifter.

But when Andrew took Peter to meet Jesus as the Christ and when Peter awakened because of the Light in this man, it altered his consciousness. His consciousness was changed as the Light was placed with him. Jesus had the ability to become a clear channel for the Holy Spirit, for the Light. He could open up and just let it flood through him, through his very beingness. With his every breath, his entire countenance could radiate Light.

Jesus of himself did nothing. He said, in essence, "Of myself, I can do nothing. It is the Father that works through me—the Spirit."[3] It is the Spirit that comes through and alters. When this Light was awakened in Peter, he went from shifting sand to solid rock. This firmness and solidity, the strength and power that is the Light, were brought into the consciousness of Peter. Peter came forward as the first apostle; Andrew, as the second.

3. John 5:19, 30

James

Then there was James, the son of Zebedee and the brother of John. James was the showman, on stage about twenty-four hours a day in an "eight-day" week. He was always attempting to take the spotlight away from other people and placing it on himself. Today, if somebody were talking about their surgery, James would be the one who would say, "If you think *your* surgery was something, you should have seen *mine*." If someone were talking about their car having four hundred horsepower, James would be the one who would say, "Mine has five hundred." No matter what you had, his seemed to be better; no matter what you did, he could do better. He was extremely self-centered, and the sun rose and set on his own thoughts about himself. Everything had to be "me first." He would sacrifice the greatest or the least for himself and, consequently, his own conscious awareness.

We could probably say that James was the perfectly selfish person. Yet when Jesus came to him and called him and when the Light of the Christ and the Holy Spirit came through him, James gave up all those things that were no longer needed. He couldn't seem to give them up before, but now they were excess baggage. He went from perfect selfishness to perfect sacrifice. Then he spread the Light everywhere, instead of just pulling it to himself. Rather than make himself the center of attention, he was able to sit back and allow other people the Light to express themselves. He didn't throw anything away; he just directed into a higher level of consciousness where he was able to express himself much more than he ever could have by restricting his expression to the physical body.

I think each person has to ask himself or herself, "Can I move from self-centeredness to self-sacrifice? Can I really stop controlling people physically, emotionally, and mentally and allow them the freedom to express themselves? Do I constantly have to make the universe revolve around my ego? Or can I step out and revolve around the universe? Can I revolve around somebody else's consciousness? Can I allow others the right to think and do whatever they want, and can I accept it and cooperate with it?" Many times, it's hard to come into this consciousness, but it is possible.

John

The fourth disciple was John. He manifested the consciousness of love—at first, the negative aspect of possessive love and, later, the positive aspect of pure spiritual love. John, God bless him, was so much in love with the Light, and it was so much a part of his life, that he wanted everybody to have it whether they wanted it or not. That's a type of love, but it's a controlling love: "You are going to get the Light whether you like it or not, and if you don't, you're no good and not worth being saved."

Jesus and the disciples were traveling around the country—this band of anarchists and rebels, as they were called by many people—and they approached a city where Jesus was to preach. The townspeople said, "No, you get out of here. We don't want you in our city. When you come and talk, we have trouble with the government; the pressures come on us. You bring us trouble. Go away."

The whole town rejected the Christ, and John was very upset by this. He said, "Let's call down the fires of heaven on these people and destroy them. They don't deserve to hear you speak. Let's destroy them right now, Jesus, you and I."

Jesus said, "No, we can't do that because perfect love says that whether they love us or not, we still must love them for the highest good of all mankind." Jesus' ability to contain the wrath of these people toward him—his saying, "It doesn't matter," and, in essence, turning the other cheek as he walked away—brought John from the temper that he had manifested to the quality of tenderness. John's love was changed through this action of the Christ Light and became strength in love, humility in love, and self-sacrifice in love. John exemplified and encompassed the consciousnesses of *all* disciples through his consciousness of divine love.

John was a constant companion of Jesus and was closer to him in the understanding of perfect love than any of the other disciples. He was called John the Beloved. All the trials and tribulations that Jesus manifested in his consciousness were manifested, also, in the consciousness of John. The one who suffered the most at the time of the crucifixion was probably John, the constant companion who was one of the inner circle—Peter, James, and John, the three who worked as the focal point of the Light as it came through Jesus, who "held" the Light for him. Jesus shared his thoughts openly with this man, John, and they became so close in this greater Light. John was one of the first, after Jesus, who became a Mystical Traveler. He had the ability to flow with the Light as it came through Jesus, and because of this, they were, indeed, spiritual brothers.

The great lesson that John brought forward was demonstrated after the crucifixion. When he had lost the physical manifestation of the master force with which he worked (Jesus), he was able to recover those broken bonds of affection and weave them into new patterns of healing and understanding. He must have been a great person to have been so close to the greatness of the Christ, as it manifested through Jesus, and then to have given it up, stepped forward, and again manifested it through these new dimensions of his consciousness. He was able to say, "Even though you are not here to show that it was a perfect love, we'll go on in this love and toward the perfection of love."

John was able to lift into a higher consciousness. Sitting on a rock and moping would have shown a selfish love. It would have shown that he loved the man, Jesus, but not the consciousness of the Christ. So John's ability to move ahead and move on showed that the Light really was there and working. He demonstrated for all of us that when we lose somebody whom we have loved, upon whom we have based our life, and who has been our foundation and our strength, this force of Light can come through and weave our love back into new and greater patterns of healing and understanding, not only for ourselves but also for other people. Just to be able to stand and say, "I understand what you are going through," is sometimes enough to lift others and give them the strength to go on.

Philip

Philip was a horse trader. He was very analytical, a little slow in his thinking, and slow to follow, and with his analytical mind, he looked before he leaped. Philip wondered what was going on with this man, Jesus. Philip was interested in ideas, but he was pragmatic: "If it's any good, it has to work. If it doesn't work, it can't be too good. And if it works, let's see it work."

Philip had some pretty set ideas about how things should be run. He had been a little critical of the way Jesus walked from city to city and wanted to put the company on horseback and make it a magnificent thing. It was almost as if he were waiting for Jesus to ask him about the horses, and then he would say, "Well, I'll give you the horses if I can be one of the group"—because he was one who bargained.

Yet when Philip came to the Son of man and Jesus reached out and touched him with the Light, Philip went from inquiry to insight. Immediately, he was aware of what was going on. This insight came forward in him, and he perceived the Light and the Christ action. This is another way we can see what the Christ is, what the Light is: we can see the way it has influenced many people.

Nathanael

Nathanael, whom we also call Bartholomew, was the sixth one called. Nathanael was a prejudiced one; when he heard that Jesus was from Nazareth, he said, "Can anything good come out of Nazareth?"[4] He had prejudged Jesus even before he met him. In advance, he "knew" in his mind that Nazareth was the lowest area around and that nothing that was any good could come from there. Yet when Jesus saw Nathanael coming toward him, he said, "Behold, an Israelite indeed, in whom is no guile!"[5]

Jesus was so honest and straightforward, and Nathanael was able to perceive the truth, the honesty, and the purity of the Christ because the Light opened his eyes. At first, it might have been difficult for him to see it in anybody else from that town, but the Light opened his eyes so that he could see it with this one man, Jesus. When the Light came upon him, Nathanael went from prejudice to purity. He no longer prejudged, and his attitude became one of observation and acceptance.

4. John 1:46 (Revised Standard Version)
5. John 1:47 (Revised Standard Version)

Thomas

Thomas was a doubter. He joined the brotherhood and became a part of the ministry of Jesus, traveling with them. Jesus taught him about the Light in special sessions, and Thomas still doubted it. All the time he was sitting with them, this consciousness would not release him, and he doubted the Light. He had to be shown. Jesus also knew this and showed him.

Thomas had walked in the brotherhood for almost three years, had watched Jesus heal people, and had watched him perform miracles. Yet, after the crucifixion, when Jesus appeared to the disciples, Thomas said, "I still doubt it." After seeing, he still doubted, but Jesus understood this consciousness of Thomas and allowed him to inspect his wounds.

It was at that moment, when Thomas was given proof that the Christ had resurrected and was there with them, that the Light was finally placed upon him, and Thomas went from doubt to dedication. He went forward and preached some of the most beautiful gospel messages from the Spirit. He was really quite a man, very forceful and strong. And remember that the Holy Spirit, the power, flowed through each one of these men—in varying degrees of consciousness, but through each one of them.

Matthew

Matthew was, in his time, a despised publican, a tax collector. Tax collectors were probably the most despised people in all Judea. They "feathered their own nests"; they would collect for the Roman government, but they'd collect a little extra for themselves. They financially subjugated mankind—and, still, Jesus chose one of them as a disciple. He chose one looked upon by many as being one of the very lowest in the land, to be elevated in consciousness. But look at the wit of the Light, to be able with the power of the spoken word to turn someone from an oppressor of mankind to one who works to free mankind.

Matthew was an excellent businessman. He knew all the angles and how to get the most for himself. He knew how to scheme, connive, and cheat, and he was very clever and wealthy. He had been using his fellow human beings to get ahead. He had been getting a fast buck any way he could, at anyone's expense, and he gave it all up when the Holy Spirit came through him and altered his consciousness.

Matthew had watched Jesus and his disciples traveling back and forth for quite some time, and he had watched them change and grow. So when Jesus said to him, "Come and follow me," Matthew jumped up from behind his tax-collecting table and followed, just like that.

When he gave up being a publican, Matthew called all his old friends together and gave them a feast. He said, "I want you to meet Jesus, the Christ, the master that I follow." He didn't even hesitate for a second, once he was called. We could say that Matthew went from the consciousness of the businessman to the consciousness of brotherhood. He gave up all his wealth to follow Jesus. He took his business mind into the brotherhood and kept track of all their money, and he kept very accurate records. It is said that Matthew recorded the Sermon on the Mount.

Thaddaeus

James

There is not too much said about Thaddaeus and James, the son of Alphaeus. They were the silent Light bearers, the ones who kept their silence. Whenever Peter, James, and John were out preaching and healing the multitudes, these two, James and Thaddaeus, held the Light similarly to a charged battery, a reservoir of power. They supported Jesus and the disciples in everything they did, and in their quiet way, they did tremendous work that most people may never know about. They never asked for recognition in any way, yet there they were, very high and very capable. And they went from silence to sainthood.

Simon

The eleventh disciple is Simon. Simon was quite an athlete. He could nimbly climb buildings, run, and jump; he was very agile. Simon was also a rabble-rouser, one of the Zealots, and he had killed more Roman soldiers than you can imagine. In our modern terminology, we might say he was a murderer.

I think Simon probably joined the company of Jesus because he thought that Jesus was someone who would overthrow the government and set up a "correct" form of government for Judea. Can you imagine the feelings he might have had when Jesus said, "My kingdom is not of this world"?[6] Can you imagine him sitting by Jesus and saying, "Where is your kingdom, Lord? If it's not here, where is it?" And can you imagine Jesus taking him on a spiritual trip into the inner realms of Light and saying, "Look, Simon, here are the realms of Light—the astral, the causal, the mental, the etheric, the Soul, and pure Spirit; this is our kingdom"?

When the Light was placed with Simon, he went from what we might call patriotism to evangelism, and he used the same fervor of his patriotism to become an evangelical speaker. He converted multitudes. No wonder he could preach a fantastic sermon; he knew where he was coming from, where he was going, and how to get there because he had been given certain keys and had seen what the kingdom is. He preached some of the most beautiful lessons of the Holy Spirit that you could ever want to hear. He could speak in tongues, interpret tongues, heal with the spoken word, cast out devils, and free the body and the mind of the negativity that people had gathered around themselves. He was really a fantastic man.

6. John 18:36 (King James Version)

Many of the disciples had belonged to rebel groups, which were in their heyday at that time. Many people were trying to overthrow the Roman government, trying to reestablish their own kingdoms. Today we would probably call them anarchists, rioters, and a lot of other things. That was what they were called at that time, too.

To understand why Jesus appeared to be a threat to the leaders of these factions, all we have to do is move into Herod's frame of reference and look at this action from his point of view or to move our consciousness to that of a Pharisee or a Sadducee. Their position is easy to understand. Most of us have identified ourselves with Jesus the Christ and have seen how he was maligned and abused, but in the few short years of his ministry, he had more followers come into his way of thinking than all the rest of the leaders put together. That's why he was a threat. He was changing the consciousness of the people, and the leaders felt this.

Judas

Then we come to Judas. The name Judas means "praise to God," and there were a lot of youngsters born during that time who were named Judas. In the Bible, this disciple is called Judas Iscariot to identify him because there were so many named Judas.

Judas may have been the greatest disciple because he sacrificed more than all the others together. We might not remember the names of all the other disciples, but we all know Judas. He came forward to betray the Son of man, to assist in setting forth a kingdom of eternal progression. This action had to take place to bring forward the greater Light in this current dispensation. Judas fulfilled destiny then so that we can fulfill our destiny now based upon his action.

During the Last Supper, Jesus said to Judas, "What you are going to do, do quickly."[7] Jesus might have added that if Judas didn't, he (Jesus) might not resurrect as the living Christ. Jesus had to have somebody he could depend on. I don't know if I would have done that. Somebody once asked me where I thought Judas is now. I said, "I think Judas, one second after he died, was in the highest heaven in God's arms because God forgave him instantly."

If people receive a choice on the inner planes (and certainly the elect Souls of this time do) to come in and manifest consciousness through the body and work out plans, then Judas chose to come forward and have his name damned through eternity as the betrayer of the action of Jesus Christ. None of the others volunteered to come forward and allow themselves to be damned down through history.

7. John 13:27 (Revised Standard Version)

In the physical embodiment, Judas had a choice and could have fulfilled the pattern with a different action of the mind. However, Judas had a resentful streak in him. For example, when Christ was having his feet anointed with oil, Judas rebuked the one who was doing this. Then, when Christ rebuked Judas, Judas felt resentful. But Christ also rebuked Peter, but Peter stayed in line and manifested the Spirit. Judas stepped out of line and manifested resentment. He had a choice, and he exercised it.

Judas often felt separated from the rest of the disciples, from the brotherhood. He felt he should be as close to Jesus as Peter, James, and John were, but he was one of the "outer" circle. All the other disciples could sit closer to Jesus than Judas could. He was on the outskirts. The others pushed him back, or, rather, he felt that they did. They were all from one city, one area, and Judas was called from another area. He felt very much the outcast, and he harbored resentment within his consciousness. Because of this, he went from resentment to ruin to revelation.

Judas knew that Jesus was the Son of God, but he was afraid that Jesus was not going to accept the throne of Judea and establish the kingdom. Judas believed wholeheartedly that the kingdom was to be here on the earth, and he was dedicated to bringing it forward. He didn't know what was really going on, yet he still fulfilled the destiny.

Judas wanted everybody to recognize Jesus as the Son of God, the Messiah, and he thought he could force Jesus to manifest his divinity and his glory and establish his kingdom on earth. So he went to the enemies of Jesus to tell them about him. As far as they were concerned, this was betrayal: "Here's the money. Point him out to us." But Judas was thinking, "When I point him out to you, he's going to show you a thing or two. He's really going to manifest that he is the king."

However, Judas was overshadowed by Satan. Through Satan, greed appeared in Judas. Whenever we manifest greed, an imbalance appears in our lives. We lose track of what we are really to do because our desire patterns go out of bounds. If Judas could have held out longer, I speculate that he could have manifested the consciousness of Thomas and gone to dedication instead of hanging himself. He could have vindicated his name and his action by going into the spiritual aspect and bringing forth the greater Light for all to see.

Jesus the Christ walked as a God-force. Judas betrayed him, and Jesus was crucified, but this couldn't have happened unless the Holy Spirit had allowed it to take place. When he was brought before Pilate, Jesus said, in essence, "You have no power over me except what is given to you by my Father. You couldn't do this to me unless my Father allowed it. You are nothing, and you can't harm me. My Father could bring angels and surround me." Many people knew this was true because Jesus had demonstrated his mastership in so many ways. Because the crucifixion was allowed by the Father, it did take place.

Judas was the instrument to bring forth the action that would manifest the Christ through the then-known range of all consciousnesses, through all realms of Light. But Judas fulfilled another destiny that everyone must realize: when you strike against the Light, you strike out. By his action, Judas said, "Don't do this. It destroys you. It must come back at you."

The more a person is attuned to the Light, the faster an action will come back to be balanced because there can be no bondage held against anyone by the Light. The Light will remove bondage immediately. If you're having disturbances with somebody and you try to forget them, the next day they may be "up in your face" for you to handle them so you can be free. This is what the Light does. It clears situations and brings them into balance rapidly. This is why we say that if something disturbs you, clear it now. Place it in the Light and clear it; balance the action so you're free.

Jesus

2

The Christ Action

The action of the Christ was reflected through the action of the disciples. The ability of Jesus to work with the Light—to bring it through to his disciples so it could alter their consciousnesses—demonstrated that he was indeed the Christ, that he was able to manifest the consciousness of the Christ. We know that the common denominator for the company of Jesus was the Holy Spirit, that power which reached in and wove them together to set up one of the greatest forces of humankind: twelve people, dedicated, who altered history.

The Christ, manifesting through Jesus, brought the Light through to each one of the disciples and brought about those changes in their consciousnesses that lifted them into the consciousness of one, the one that we all know, who is the Christ. We *know* this, and flesh and blood doesn't reveal it to us. The Father who is in heaven, the inner Spirit, testifies to this in each of us.

The miracles of Jesus were not really miracles in the sense that they were unrepeatable. He said, "He who believes in me will also do the works that I do; and greater works than these will he do, because I go to the Father."[8] Jesus promised this to us. He made us heirs to his kingdom of Light—not the worlds of illusion, but the pure realms of the Spirit. Each one of us will inherit the throne if we follow the Light and the way of the Light, which is the Holy Spirit.

I think that each of us has manifested to some degree or another or do manifest the consciousnesses of these disciples. At one time we may be shifting, and then we become solid. Sometimes we doubt, and sometimes we are firm in our faith and knowledge. Sometimes we are silent, and sometimes we can teach a beautiful lesson of Light to others. If we have a chance to manifest the consciousness of any of the disciples, then we might want to choose to express the positive aspects—the dedication, the brotherhood, the sacrifice, the divine love, the purity, the power of the Light, and the humility that allows us to accept the Light and work within the action of the Christ.

8. John 14:12 (Revised Standard Version)

The
Cosmic
Christ
Calendar

I'd like to share some information about the esoteric or the Cosmic Christ, the one that is like oxygen or air. You don't have to like or dislike air; you breathe it without even thinking about it. It sustains life. The Cosmic Christ is like that; it sustains life. It is present, totally, at every moment. It can't be copyrighted or catalogued or categorized. It can, however, be personalized through various ways that I want to share with you.

There are so many ways to approach a concept of Christ that the airwaves are filled with it. The churches are filled with it. Not too many, however, want to discuss a process of *going to Christ*. Far too many want to sit down and let Christ come to them. That's fine, if it works, and for some that is happening. But for the greater majority, it just isn't happening. Perhaps the way to know the Cosmic Christ is to make a commitment towards that, as a focal point of our own directed energy, rather than as a vague theory that we occasionally listen to someone else discuss.

Perhaps the time is present when we can take direction of our own lives, in accordance with the Father's will, and move ourselves in the direction of the Cosmic Christ.

Christmas actually extends from the last week of November to January 6. Then there are four weeks after that, the time of the Epiphany. This whole season can be a time when you recommit to becoming more aware of the Christ Consciousness within you.

To help you, there are focus statements for the weeks leading up to Christmas day. You can meditate on these ideas and look for ways you can express them in your everyday life.

From that point, there are meditations for each day through January 6, along with the name of the apostle and the zodiac sign for each day, as well as other information. You might want to find your zodiac sign and consider that day your "high holy day of meditation."

For the four weeks of the Epiphany, there are weekly dedications, actions, and affirmations that you can use to anchor your learnings of the Christmas season and to assist you in living the Christ Consciousness in a greater way.

November 28 to December 4

The *Annunciation* week is a time to cultivate purity in your life. You enter into the purification process through your loving. When your total loving is present, there's not too much room for anything else.

December 5 to December 11

The week of the *Immaculate Conception* is a time when everything you conceive is done in terms of God being entirely present. All dis-ease is done away with because nothing that is impure can reside in the presence of God.

December 12 to December 18

The week of the *Holy Birth* is a time for bringing into the world that which is pure, loving, and of the Christed nature.

December 19 to December 25

This is the week of the *Christ Consciousness* manifesting its presence. With that presence comes cleansing, purity, and peace. The illumination of this moment is blessed by God, personally, and is recognized as God's hand with you in the physical form. God's glory births itself, and you become the vehicle for that expression.

December 24

Christmas Eve is the night when "angels" touch the earth with their hearts, and the radiant energies of Spirit come pouring through.

December 25

Christmas Day is a time when we can see things more clearly than ever before.

On that first Christmas day, when Jesus was born, his mother, Mary, represented the female principle, and Joseph represented the male principle. Those two principles blended into the oneness of the Christ. So we have both the male and the female and the clear God consciousness—manifested as the Christ. It's a very simple thing.

The manger in which Christ Jesus was born is another simple statement, which says, "You start from where you are." You don't have to get to some elevated position to start. You don't have to be enthroned in order to say, "Now I'll grow." You grow from where you are. If you're experiencing doubt and despair, you don't have to wait until you're clear to start. You start right where you are, right now. It's really nice to know that this is just the way it is.

The
Twelve Days
of
Christmas

December 26

James

Apostle: James

Zodiac sign: Aries

Home of: The Zeophim, and the Elohim (the lords of creation)

Cosmic pattern: The perfect earth above the world; the ideal

Center of power: Head

Musical keynote: B-flat major

Composers: Bach, Rachmaninoff, Haydn

Meditation: Behold, I make all thing new.

December 27

Andrew

Apostle: Andrew

Zodiac sign: Taurus

Home of: The Tetraphim

Cosmic pattern: The perfected form

Center of power: Throat

Musical keynote: E-flat major

Composer: Tchaikovsky

Meditation: He that dwelleth in love dwelleth in God.

December 28

Thomas

Apostle: Thomas
Zodiac sign: Gemini
Home of: The Seraphim
Cosmic pattern: Great peace
Center of power: Hands
Musical keynote: F-sharp major
Composers: Grieg, Wagner, Gounod
Meditation: Be still and know that I am God.

December 29

Nathanael

Apostle: Nathanael (Bartholomew)

Zodiac sign: Cancer

Home of: The Cherubim

Cosmic pattern: Intuition, the divine feminine principle

Center of power: Solar plexus

Musical keynote: G-sharp major

Composer: Mahler

Meditation: If we walk in the Light as he is in the Light, we have fellowship with each other.

December 30

Judas

Apostle: Judas
Zodiac sign: Leo
Home of: The Lords of the Flame
Cosmic pattern: The power of love
Center of power: Heart
Musical keynote: A-sharp major
Composer: Debussy
Meditation: Love is the fulfilling of the Law.

December 31

James

Apostle: James, son of Alphaeus

Zodiac sign: Virgo

Home of: The Lords of Wisdom and Service

Cosmic pattern: A cleansed and rejuvenated earth

Center of power: Intestinal tract

Musical keynote: F major

Composer: Meyerbeer

Meditation: He that is greatest among you shall be your servant.

January 1

Thaddaeus

Apostle: Thaddaeus (Jude)
Zodiac sign: Libra
Home of: The Lords of Individuality
Cosmic pattern: Make the world beautiful; keep it in
    balance
Center of power: Adrenal glands
Musical keynote: D major
Composer: Verdi
Meditation: Ye shall know the truth, and the truth
    shall set you free.

January 2

John

Apostle: John

Zodiac sign: Scorpio

Home: The Lords of Form

Cosmic pattern: Attainment by the transmutation of matter into Spirit

Center of power: Regenerative system

Musical keynote: E major

Composer: Liszt

Meditation: Blessed are the pure in heart, for they shall see God.

January 3

Philip

Apostle: Philip
Zodiac sign: Sagittarius
Home of: The Lords of the Mind
Cosmic pattern: All earth is an altar of peace.
Center of power: Stomach
Musical keynote: F major
Composer: Beethoven
Meditation: Ye are the Light of the world.

January 4

Simon

Apostle: Simon
Zodiac sign: Capricorn
Home of: The Archangels
Cosmic pattern: The Christ shall reign personally
  upon the earth in all mankind
Center of power: Knees
Musical keynote: G major
Composer: Puccini
Meditation: Let the Christ be born in you.

January 5

Matthew

Apostle: Matthew

Zodiac sign: Aquarius

Home of: The Angels

Cosmic pattern: The Fatherhood of God and the brotherhood of man

Center of power: The two lower limbs

Musical keynote: A major

Composers: Schubert, Mendelssohn, Mozart

Meditation: Ye are my friends.

January 6

Peter

Apostle: Peter

Zodiac sign: Pisces

Home of: The Earth Masters and the Lords of Compassion

Cosmic pattern: The perfected man

Center of power: Feet

Musical keynote: B major

Composers: Chopin, Handel, Ravel

Meditation: God created man in His own image.

The Epiphany

Jesus

The four weeks after the twelve days of Christmas are the Epiphany. It is a time for seership and a time of being the prophet, the seer, the revelator.

January 7 to January 13

Dedication: For prayer, meditation, spiritual exercises, and for giving 100-percent quality to this work

Action: The union of the body, mind, and Soul

Affirmation: I am renewing myself through all things.

January 14 to January 20

Dedication: For purity and transmutation

Action: Seeing everything through the eyes of the Christ

Affirmation: I use all things to lift me spiritually.

January 21 to January 27

Dedication: For the awakening of the spiritual mind

Action: Following through on commitments

Affirmation: My discipline is my freedom.

January 28 to February 3

Dedication: For sublimation and unification

Action: Knowing God in all things

Affirmation: I love all people through my oneness.

ABOUT THE AUTHOR

Since 1963, John-Roger has traveled all over the world, lecturing, teaching, and assisting people who want to create a life of greater health, happiness, peace, and prosperity and a greater awakening to the Spirit within. His humor and practical wisdom have benefited thousands and lightened many a heart.

In the course of this work, he has given over 4,000 seminars, many of which are televised nationally on "That Which Is.: He has also written more than 20 books, including co-authoring the *New York Times* #1 best-seller *DO IT!* and the best-selling *You Can't Afford the Luxury of a Negative Thought.*

The common thread throughout all John-Roger's work is loving, opening to the highest good of all, and the awareness that God is abundantly present and available.

If you've enjoyed this book, you may want to explore and delve more deeply into what John-Roger has shared about this subject and other related topics. For a selection of study materials and more information on John-Roger's teachings through MSIA, please contact us at:

MSIA
P.O. Box 3935
Los Angeles, CA 90051
(213) 737-4055.

The Meditation of the Christ

A beautiful Christmas eve seminar and meditation on the Christ, where J-R explains how we can prepare ourselves to receive the consciousness of the Christ.
#1329 $10 Audio

Christ Is Forgiveness

An Easter seminar, in which J-R speaks of Jesus' life and explains that the essence of the Christ is forgiveness.
#7287 $10 Audio; #V-7287 $20 Video

The Anointed One

Five audio tapes focusing on the Christ. Includes the moving and powerful "Christ Innerphasing," outstanding excerpts on "God, Traveler, Christ, You," and "The Inner Christ" seminar. A beautiful collection.
#3906 $35 Audio Tape Packet